Title Page

The AI-Powered Mechanic: Mastering Prompts for Heavy Equipment Success
Leverage Artificial Intelligence to Diagnose Faster, Learn Smarter, and Boost Your Efficiency
By Saul Werkmann

Table of Contents

Formatting for KDP Submission

Recommended KDP Formatting Standards:

- **Book Dimensions:** 6" x 9"
- **Margins:** 0.75" margins (standard KDP template)
- **Font and Size:** Times New Roman, 12-point
- **Line Spacing:** 1.15 line spacing
- **Chapter Titles:** Bold, font size 16–18pt
- **Subtitles:** Italics, 14pt
- **Body Text:** Justified alignment

When ready to publish, paste this fully formatted content into your preferred word-processing software (Microsoft Word, Google Docs), ensure all images and diagrams (if any) are properly formatted, and export as a PDF optimized for KDP upload. Use the KDP online preview tool to verify the final layout before publication.

[Full chapter content begins on the next page.]

[Full content inserted below.]

Chapter 1: Why AI? Why Now?

Heavy equipment has come a long way from the days of steam engines and purely mechanical linkages. Today's machines are a complex blend of hydraulics, electronics, sensors, and software. As the industry evolves, so must the technicians who maintain and repair these machines. That's where Artificial Intelligence (AI) comes in.

AI isn't just a futuristic concept. It's already here—helping businesses streamline logistics, doctors make faster diagnoses, and even powering the voice assistants in our pockets. Now, it's making its way into the heavy equipment world, not just through onboard systems, but also as a powerful assistant in your repair process.

The Problem with Modern Repair Work

Modern diagnostics can be overwhelming:

- Fault codes with cryptic descriptions
- Dozens of system interactions
- OEM procedures locked behind portals or buried in PDFs
- Inconsistent or outdated information from search engines

Mechanics often waste valuable time:

- Clicking through forums full of guesses
- Reading 40-page PDFs to find one torque spec
- Repeating repairs because a root cause was missed

AI helps solve that problem by cutting through the noise.

What AI Can Do for You

AI tools like ChatGPT and Claude can:

- Summarize service manuals into bullet points
- Explain complex systems in plain English
- Help you draft checklists, estimates, or reports
- Identify likely causes of symptoms based on your description

What This Book Offers

This book is your guide to mastering AI tools as a heavy equipment mechanic. It will show you how to:

- Write effective prompts that get useful answers
- Use AI to troubleshoot, research, and explain repairs
- Integrate AI into your workflow without relying on it blindly

You don't need to be a computer expert. You just need to be curious, open-minded, and ready to add another powerful tool to your belt.

If you've ever wished you had a fast, knowledgeable assistant who never gets tired and can explain anything in seconds—AI is it.

Let's dive in and explore how it can change your work for the better.

Chapter Questions:

1. What problems in modern repair work can AI help reduce?
2. Name three things AI tools can assist mechanics with.
3. Why is it important for today's mechanics to understand AI?

Chapter 2: Understanding Your AI Assistant (Simplified)

Artificial Intelligence, particularly in the form of Large Language Models (LLMs), can seem intimidating at first glance. However, once demystified, it becomes clear that AI functions much like a highly sophisticated pattern recognition system. To truly leverage AI effectively, especially as a heavy equipment mechanic, you need to understand how these AI models operate.

What is a Large Language Model (LLM)?

An LLM is a software system trained on billions of words pulled from the internet, manuals, books, technical documentation, and more. Instead of memorizing facts, the AI learns the patterns in how words and concepts are used together. When you ask it a question—known as a prompt—it uses these patterns to generate a likely response.

LLMs are not connected to live databases. They can't pull live codes or access your machine's telematics. However, they can recall likely meanings of diagnostic codes, outline repair procedures, or help explain a system you're not familiar with—based on what it has "read."

How Prompts Work

AI responses are generated based on your prompt. The better your prompt, the better your answer. For example, instead of saying "Why is my machine overheating?" you might say:

"Act as a John Deere service technician. My machine is a 2018 John Deere 210G excavator. It runs hot during heavy digging but doesn't throw any codes. Radiator is clean. Hydraulics are responsive. Please list 5 possible causes."

This kind of detailed prompt gives the AI direction, context, and an expected format. In response, it might suggest things like:

- Cooling fan not engaging fully
- Thermostat sticking
- Internal hydraulic bypass heating the system
- EGR cooler restriction
- Faulty temperature sensor giving incorrect readings

The AI didn't read your machine—it predicted this based on patterns in its training data. It's fast, useful, and directional—but not a replacement for actual tests.

Strengths and Weaknesses of AI

Strengths:

- Extremely fast at summarizing long manuals or finding potential faults based on symptoms
- Can explain complex systems in simple terms
- Great for brainstorming diagnostic paths
- Helps draft reports, generate checklists, or compare systems quickly

Weaknesses:

- It can hallucinate—confidently making things up
- It doesn't know if a part number is still valid
- It has no awareness of recent service bulletins unless you paste them in
- It does not understand your exact machine or setup

Where AI Fits In

Think of AI as a powerful shop assistant. It won't replace your tools, but it will help you:

- Learn a new system faster
- Clarify strange fault codes
- Draft a service estimate
- Outline the steps for a rare repair you've never done

It's especially useful when you're stuck and want to hear possible causes. It helps narrow your focus or gives you the right terms to search for in a manual or parts catalog.

Use it wisely, and it will become one of your most valuable tools.

Chapter Questions:

1. How does an AI Large Language Model generate responses?
2. What is a primary limitation of AI-generated responses?
3. Why is the quality of your prompt crucial to receiving useful information?

Chapter Questions:

1. How does an AI Large Language Model generate responses?
2. What is a primary limitation of AI-generated responses?
3. Why is the quality of your prompt crucial to receiving useful information?

Chapter 3: The Anatomy of an Effective Prompt

Crafting an effective prompt is like writing a detailed work order for your smartest helper. The more specific and focused your request, the better the results you get. AI is not a mind reader—it only works with what you give it.

The Four Key Elements of an Effective Prompt

To consistently get quality responses from AI, include these four pieces:

1. Role or Persona: Tell the AI who to act as.

- Example: "Act as a Komatsu hydraulic specialist."

2. Action / Task: Be clear about what you want it to do.

- Example: "List 5 potential causes of..." or "Explain how..."

3. Detailed Context: Include machine make, model, year, system, symptoms, fault codes, hours, environmental conditions, recent work, etc.

- Example: "Komatsu PC290LC-11, 6,300 hours, slow swing only when warm."

4. Output Format: Ask for the information in a way that's useful.

- Example: "In a bullet list, ranked from most to least likely."

Why Vague Prompts Fail

If you ask: "Why does my excavator bog down?"
AI doesn't know:

- What kind of excavator
- If it's under load
- If it's been serviced
- What "bog down" means in this context

So it'll give a generic answer: "Low fuel pressure, clogged filters, pump issue, load too high."

Instead, try:

"Act as a Case equipment engine technician. My 2016 Case CX250D (Tier 4) has a bogging issue when the hydraulic functions are active. Fuel filters replaced last week. Engine revs fine in neutral. Please provide likely causes in a checklist format."

Now you'll get a list that actually fits your situation.

More Examples

Prompt A:
"Summarize this 2-page service bulletin."

Prompt B:
"Create a checklist for daily inspection on a CAT 950M loader used in freezing conditions."

Prompt C:
"Explain how a regen system works on a John Deere 644K. Use simple terms for a new apprentice."

Each of these is precise, actionable, and gives AI a role, a task, and clear expectations.

Prompting is a Skill

Just like learning to run diagnostics or trace a wiring issue, writing good prompts takes practice. Use the SPEC method (coming in Chapter 4) to guide you every time you use AI.

Treat every prompt like you're giving instructions to a smart assistant who's never seen your machine—but knows a lot of general patterns.

Chapter Questions:

1. What four elements constitute a highly effective prompt?
2. How can context improve AI's response accuracy?
3. Why is specifying output format important in prompt writing?

Chapter Questions:

1. What four elements constitute a highly effective prompt?
2. How can context improve AI's response accuracy?
3. Why is specifying output format important in prompt writing?

Chapter 4: The Prompt Engineering Framework (SPEC Method)

Now that you understand the anatomy of an effective prompt, let's make it easier to apply. The SPEC Method is a simple memory aid designed for mechanics who need a consistent, quick way to structure prompts—especially in the middle of a busy shift.

SPEC stands for:

- **S**pecify machine and system
- **P**resent the problem or symptoms
- **E**laborate with important context
- **C**ommand a clear action and output format

Let's walk through each element:

S – Specify Machine & System

This is where you tell the AI exactly what type of equipment and system you're dealing with. Include:

- Manufacturer (e.g., CAT, Komatsu, Deere, Case)

- Model (e.g., CAT 336, JD 450K)
- System (e.g., hydraulics, electrical, aftertreatment)
- Example: "Komatsu PC210LC-10, boom hydraulic circuit."

Without this, the AI might give you suggestions for a totally unrelated system.

P – Present the Problem/Symptoms

Next, describe what's going wrong. Be precise:

- What's happening?
- When does it happen?
- Are there any fault codes?
- Example: "Boom-up function is slow, especially when warm. All other hydraulic functions work normally. No active fault codes."

Avoid vague terms like "something's wrong" or "weird issue."

E – Elaborate with Important Context

This is where you give background info:

- Machine hours
- Recent maintenance
- Environmental conditions
- Operating load
- Example: "Machine has 7,900 hours. Hydraulic oil and filters were changed 100 hours ago. Issue began after cleaning around the hydraulic manifold with a pressure washer."

Even if the AI doesn't have real-time awareness, it will use this detail to tailor suggestions more intelligently.

C – Command a Clear Action and Format

What do you want the AI to do?

- List causes?
- Explain how something works?
- Generate a procedure?

Also, tell it how to present the answer:

- Bullet points
- Checklist
- Ranked list
- Table format

Example: "List the top 5 possible causes for the slow boom-up, ranked from most to least likely, and include a one-line test/check for each."

Putting It All Together

Here's a full prompt using SPEC:

"Act as a Komatsu hydraulic technician. My machine is a Komatsu PC210LC-10, with 7,900 hours. The boom-up function is noticeably slow, especially when warm. All other hydraulic functions operate normally. No codes are present. Hydraulic fluid and filters changed recently. This issue started after a pressure wash. Please list the top 5 likely causes in ranked order. Include one brief diagnostic test per cause."

This is SPEC in action—and it gets you a highly targeted, useful answer.

Fast SPEC Prompt Template

Act as a [Specialist Type]. Machine: [Make, Model, Year]. System: [e.g., hydraulics]. Symptom: [detailed description]. Context: [hours, recent work, conditions]. Task: [What do you want?] Format: [bullet list, checklist, etc.]

Practice Makes Perfect

Try writing a few SPEC prompts on recent issues you've dealt with. Test them with your favorite AI model. You'll notice that good prompts lead to good answers—and poor ones lead to frustrating output.

With repetition, SPEC becomes second nature and boosts your ability to use AI as a diagnostic companion.

Chapter Questions:

1. What does each letter of SPEC represent?
2. Provide a full SPEC-style example for a no-start issue.
3. Why is it important to include context and command in AI prompts?

Chapter Questions:

1. What does each letter of SPEC represent?
2. Provide a full SPEC-style example for a no-start issue.
3. Why is it important to include context and command in AI prompts?

Chapter 5: Advanced Prompting Techniques

Once you've mastered the basics of prompt structure and the SPEC method, it's time to take things further. The following techniques will help you use AI more like a diagnostic partner—able to reason, refine, and support your repair strategy.

1. Iterative Prompting

AI isn't a one-shot tool. You can go back and forth with it to get better answers.

Start simple:

"List 5 causes for no-crank in a CAT 420F backhoe."

Follow up:

"Assume battery is new and terminals are clean. What's next most likely?"

Refine further:

"If relay clicks but starter doesn't engage, what next?"

This back-and-forth helps narrow the issue, especially in tricky electrical problems.

2. Chain-of-Thought Reasoning

Sometimes it helps to force the AI to think step-by-step. You can say:

"Think through this step by step. How would a faulty joystick sensor cause intermittent swing control on a Case CX210C?"

This style of prompting helps break down causes and connections.

3. Request Simple Explanations (ELI5 Style)

When you're training an apprentice or brushing up on a system yourself, ask the AI to explain things simply:

"Explain the difference between a closed center and open center hydraulic system like I'm a new tech."
"Use plain terms. Don't get too technical."

You can also ask for analogies or comparisons to help clarify.

4. Prompt for Comparison

AI is great at comparisons when you're deciding between tools, methods, or designs.

Example Prompt:

"Compare the advantages and disadvantages of wet disc brakes versus dry drum brakes in off-road haul trucks."

Example Format:

"Put it in a table with Pros/Cons."

5. Summarization

Have a long technical bulletin, PDF, or OEM document?

Prompt:

"Summarize the key points of this CAT service bulletin regarding regen procedures."

You can even ask it to:

- Extract only torque specs
- Highlight safety warnings
- Pull out step-by-step sequences

6. Diagnostic Trees and Flowcharts

You can have AI generate a basic diagnostic logic tree:

Prompt:

"Create a step-by-step diagnostic flow for a Komatsu D65PX with a slow steering response."

While it won't replace a full OEM flowchart, it gives you a head start when brainstorming.

7. Hypothetical Scenario Prompting

Use this when something doesn't make sense:

"Assume there's no pressure at the test port but the pump is confirmed good. What else could explain it?"

You're guiding the AI to look outside the box.

Tip: Stack Prompts

Combine multiple techniques:

"Step-by-step, explain how a stuck proportional valve might cause a slow boom-down issue on a CAT 336. Then compare this to the effect of a weak pilot signal."

This style of prompting gets you layered, deep, and smart analysis.

Chapter Questions:

1. What is iterative prompting and why is it useful?
2. When would you use chain-of-thought reasoning with AI?
3. Give an example of how you might ask for a diagnostic flow using AI.

Chapter Questions:

1. What is iterative prompting and why is it useful?
2. When would you use chain-of-thought reasoning with AI?
3. Give an example of how you might ask for a diagnostic flow using AI.

Chapter 6: AI for Diagnostics and Troubleshooting

AI becomes a powerful tool in the hands of a mechanic who knows how to describe symptoms accurately and ask for logical troubleshooting support. Whether it's an intermittent issue or a hard fault code, AI can help you generate a list of likely causes and suggest efficient ways to test each one. This chapter shows how AI can dramatically shorten diagnostic time without skipping critical steps.

Understanding the Diagnostic Flow

Diagnosing a heavy equipment issue usually follows a familiar path:

- Identify the symptoms
- Retrieve any fault codes
- Review the system involved
- Check recent repairs or events
- Test components step-by-step

AI can assist in nearly every one of these steps. It can:

- Translate obscure fault codes
- Suggest which components are commonly involved
- Propose diagnostic tests
- Build logical sequences to eliminate root causes

Real-World Example: Intermittent Power Loss

Scenario: A John Deere 672G motor grader is reported to have intermittent power loss under load.

Prompt:

"Act as a John Deere powertrain technician. The machine is a 672G grader with 5,100 hours. The operator reports intermittent engine power loss when climbing grades or when the fan kicks in. No codes are active. Fuel filters were replaced 50 hours ago. Please list likely causes in order and suggest test procedures."

AI Output Could Include:

- Charge air cooler leak → Pressure test system
- Fuel delivery restriction → Flow test at injector rail
- Turbo actuator delay → Command test via service tool
- Fan clutch overload → Compare fan speed vs command
- ECM voltage drops → Inspect grounds and battery cables

You'd still verify all suggestions, but now you've got a place to start and a list of likely culprits.

When AI Excels

AI shines in these situations:

- No-code scenarios
- Symptoms that span multiple systems (e.g., hydraulics and electrical)
- Intermittent faults
- Non-urgent but chronic issues (e.g., slow regen, long crank, noisy hydraulic valve)

Tips for Using AI in Diagnostics

- Always provide full context (see Chapter 4's SPEC method)
- Ask for probable causes ranked by likelihood
- Ask for simple, step-by-step test procedures
- Confirm each step with OEM guidelines

Use Caution:

- AI is a suggestion engine—not a replacement for testing
- Never skip tests based on AI assumptions
- Always follow up with hands-on verification

Chapter Questions:

1. In what scenarios does AI excel in diagnostics?
2. Why is it important to give AI ranked cause lists?

3. What must you always do after receiving AI diagnostic suggestions?

Chapter Questions:

1. In what scenarios does AI excel in diagnostics?
2. Why is it important to give AI ranked cause lists?
3. What must you always do after receiving AI diagnostic suggestions?

Chapter 7: AI for Repair Procedures and Information Retrieval

Diagnostics tell you what's wrong. Repair procedures tell you how to fix it. AI can assist in writing clear, efficient repair plans, finding general procedure outlines, and summarizing complex OEM instructions. But you must verify every step with the actual OEM documentation.

Use Cases for AI in Repairs

- Drafting step-by-step guides for known repairs
- Explaining how a system comes apart (e.g., hydrostat removal)
- Estimating tool requirements and safety precautions
- Outlining proper sequence of removal/installation

Real-World Example: Water Pump Replacement

Prompt:

"Act as a CAT engine tech. Provide a detailed step-by-step guide to replace the water pump on a CAT C7 engine installed in a 2009 motor grader. Include safety precautions and torque spec reminders."

AI Response Might Include:

- Disconnect battery
- Drain coolant system
- Remove fan shroud and belt
- Unbolt and remove pump housing
- Clean mating surface
- Install new pump with fresh gasket
- Torque bolts to OEM spec (verify in CAT SIS)
- Refill coolant, bleed system, and test for leaks

Again—great draft, but double-check every step with the actual CAT service manual.

Information Retrieval

You can also use AI to:

- Summarize 50-page OEM repair PDFs
- Extract torque specs or tool lists from manuals
- Compare procedures across machine generations

Prompt:

"Summarize the differences between DPF cleaning on Tier 3 vs Tier 4B versions of the Komatsu WA380 loader."

Result: You'll get a helpful overview, which you then verify before acting.

When AI Struggles

- It may invent torque specs or step numbers
- It might skip safety warnings
- It may confuse part generations (especially if model years overlap)

Rule of Thumb:

Use AI to plan and prepare. Use OEM documentation to execute.

Chapter Questions:

1. What are three repair tasks AI can help draft procedures for?
2. Why must all AI repair steps be verified?
3. How can AI help with long OEM documents or manuals?

Chapter Questions:

1. What are three repair tasks AI can help draft procedures for?
2. Why must all AI repair steps be verified?
3. How can AI help with long OEM documents or manuals?

Chapter 8: AI for Professional Development and Skill Enhancement

Beyond troubleshooting and repairs, AI is a powerful tool for continuous learning and skill development. It can function like an on-demand tutor, mentor, or technical coach—offering simplified explanations, practice questions, and even study plans to help mechanics level up.

Why Continuous Learning Matters

Heavy equipment is constantly evolving. From emissions regulations to electronic control systems, today's machines are packed with features that didn't exist ten years ago. A mechanic who relies only on what they learned when they started is going to fall behind.

AI helps you keep pace—whether you're a veteran tech brushing up on hydraulic schematics or a new apprentice trying to understand diesel aftertreatment systems.

Using AI to Simplify Complex Topics

Prompt Examples:

- "Explain how an SCR system works in a Tier 4 Final engine like I'm a student tech."
- "Summarize the function of a pressure-compensated hydraulic pump in plain language."
- "Compare hydrostatic and powershift transmissions."

AI can rephrase technical documents into more digestible formats. You can even ask it to:

- Use analogies (e.g., compare circuits to plumbing)
- Break concepts into numbered steps
- Define acronyms and jargon

Quizzing Yourself or Others

Prompt Examples:

- "Create a 10-question quiz on CAN bus fundamentals for mechanics."
- "Give me a study guide for understanding J1939 diagnostic codes."

This is especially helpful for apprentices, test prep, or brushing up on weak areas. You can ask AI to:

- Generate flashcards
- List interview questions
- Offer multiple-choice questions with answers

Building Confidence

When you understand the why behind a system, you're more confident working on it. That confidence translates into:

- Quicker repairs
- Fewer mistakes
- Better communication with customers

AI can help you explore new systems before you ever touch them. It's like test-driving knowledge.

Practical Example: Understanding Regen Systems
Prompt:

"Explain diesel particulate filter (DPF) regeneration and the difference between passive and active regen in plain language. Include what the operator should and shouldn't do during each."

AI Might Say:

- Passive regen happens automatically at high temps.
- Active regen is initiated by the ECM when soot builds up.
- Operators should avoid shutting the machine down during active regen.

Clear, concise, and confidence-building.

Chapter Questions:

1. How can AI simplify complex mechanical systems?
2. What are some ways AI can be used for skill development?
3. Why does understanding system theory improve repair outcomes?

Chapter Questions:

1. How can AI simplify complex mechanical systems?
2. What are some ways AI can be used for skill development?
3. Why does understanding system theory improve repair outcomes?

Chapter 9: AI for Efficient Communication and Documentation

In a shop or field service environment, great mechanical skills mean nothing if you can't clearly explain the problem, the fix, and the cost. AI can help mechanics improve written communication, generate professional service notes, and prepare reports that earn customer trust.

Writing Clear Repair Summaries

AI can turn your shorthand into polished communication:

Your Notes:

"Replaced boost sensor. Found open in signal wire 2" back from ECM. Repaired. Cleared 2639. Test drive ok."

Prompt:

"Turn this into a professional repair summary for a customer invoice."

AI Output:

"Technician diagnosed an intermittent low boost pressure code. Inspection revealed an open circuit in the boost sensor signal wire approximately 2 inches from the ECM connector. The damaged section was repaired and secured. A new boost sensor was installed, and fault code 2639 was cleared. Final road test confirmed normal operation."

Generating Job Estimates or Task Lists

Prompt:

"Create a parts-and-labor estimate for replacing a final drive on a CAT 963D."

AI can give you a rough template that you refine with actual part numbers and shop rates.

Writing Safety Warnings or SOPs

Prompt:

"Write a safety checklist for removing a hydraulic cylinder from a John Deere 310SL backhoe."

Use AI to draft procedures, then edit for shop-specific protocols.

Helping with Customer Communication

Sometimes you need to break things down for a non-technical audience:

Prompt:

"Explain a regen system failure in plain terms to a fleet manager with no mechanical background."

AI can help avoid jargon, keep it brief, and highlight urgency without causing panic.

Caution: Always Proofread

AI-generated reports are fast and helpful, but always review them. Make sure:

- They match what was actually done
- There are no invented parts, steps, or specs
- The tone is professional and accurate

Chapter Questions:

1. How can AI help you turn rough notes into professional service reports?
2. Why is clear documentation important in field service work?
3. Give an example of how you might use AI to explain a repair to a customer.

Chapter Questions:

1. How can AI help you turn rough notes into professional service reports?
2. Why is clear documentation important in field service work?
3. Give an example of how you might use AI to explain a repair to a customer.

Chapter 10: Safety, Verification, and Limitations – The Golden Rules

Before we go any further, it's time to emphasize what may be the most important message in this entire book: AI is a powerful tool—but safety, verification, and human judgment come first. Always.

Rule #1: AI Is Not a Replacement for OEM Service Manuals

Every OEM (Original Equipment Manufacturer) publishes repair, maintenance, and safety manuals for a reason. AI can't replace that information. It can help summarize or interpret it, but it is never a substitute.

Always refer to the OEM manual for:

- Torque specs
- Fluid capacities
- Step-by-step procedures
- Component location diagrams

Prompt Suggestion:

"Summarize the procedure for a final drive oil change on a CAT D6T, but remind me to verify all specs with the OEM manual."

Even when the AI's output sounds correct—it must be verified.

Rule #2: Trust but Verify (Heavily on the Verify)

AI can generate:

- A missing torque spec
- An estimated fluid type
- A suggested procedure

But it can also generate completely false data that sounds real. This is called a "hallucination."

You must cross-check:

- Specs → Compare with OEM service info
- Procedures → Match against official repair guides
- Part numbers → Confirm in the correct parts catalog

Never perform work based solely on AI suggestions.

Rule #3: Safety Protocols Come First

AI might suggest useful steps, but it has no true awareness of physical danger.

ALWAYS follow safety guidelines like:

- Lockout/Tagout (LOTO)
- Hydraulic pressure relief
- Electrical system isolation
- Using proper PPE
- Proper lifting and cribbing procedures

Don't rely on AI to remind you of safety—build your own safety checklist into your workflow.

Rule #4: AI Doesn't Understand Machines—It Understands Text

AI doesn't know what your machine is doing. It hasn't smelled burnt fluid, seen a broken harness, or heard a noisy bearing.

You have to:

- Use your five senses
- Use diagnostic tools (multimeter, gauges, laptop, etc.)
- Perform hands-on testing

AI doesn't "think." It predicts language. That's very different from troubleshooting logic.

Rule #5: Be Cautious About What You Input

Many AI platforms store or review prompt data.

Avoid typing in:

- Customer names
- Machine serial numbers
- Company-sensitive information

If your shop or employer has a privacy policy—follow it strictly.

Chapter Questions:

1. Why should AI never be used as a replacement for OEM manuals?
2. What is a hallucination in the context of AI?
3. What key safety procedures must be followed regardless of AI input?

Chapter Questions:

1. Why should AI never be used as a replacement for OEM manuals?
2. What is a hallucination in the context of AI?
3. What key safety procedures must be followed regardless of AI input?

Chapter 11: Choosing Your AI Tools and Staying Current

There are dozens of AI tools available—and more appear every year. This chapter helps you choose the right ones for your needs and explains how to stay current as the technology evolves.

What to Look for in an AI Tool

When evaluating AI tools for mechanic work, look for:

- **Accuracy** – Does it return detailed, useful responses?
- **Responsiveness** – Is it fast?
- **Context depth** – Can it handle long, detailed prompts?
- **Interface** – Is it easy to use on your phone or shop computer?

Recommended Tools (as of 2025)

1. ChatGPT (OpenAI)

- Best for detailed responses, reasoning, and clarity
- Paid version (ChatGPT Plus) offers more advanced models (e.g., GPT-4)

2. Gemini (Google)

- Strong search integration, useful for summarizing online info

3. Claude (Anthropic)

- Large prompt capacity, good for long documents and context-aware outputs

4. Perplexity AI

- Great for cited responses and quick research

How to Stay Updated

AI tools are evolving monthly. To keep up:

- Bookmark the tool's official blog or changelog
- Watch YouTube or Reddit for mechanic-specific usage examples
- Join forums or Facebook groups focused on AI in trades
- Check every 3–6 months for major updates

New capabilities—like PDF uploading, image recognition, or improved voice interfaces—can make your job easier overnight.

Use Tool Variety

You don't have to pick just one AI. Use them like tools in a toolbox:

- **ChatGPT** for reasoning
- **Gemini** for web info
- **Claude** for long docs
- **Perplexity** for quick, sourced answers

Example Comparison Prompt

"Compare ChatGPT, Claude, and Gemini for summarizing a 40-page hydraulic troubleshooting manual. Rank them by clarity, speed, and accuracy."

Test a few prompts across platforms to see what fits your workflow best.

Chapter Questions:

1. What should you look for when choosing an AI tool for mechanic work?
2. Why is it important to check for updates in your chosen AI tool?
3. How can using multiple AI tools together help you?

Chapter Questions:

1. What should you look for when choosing an AI tool for mechanic work?
2. Why is it important to check for updates in your chosen AI tool?
3. How can using multiple AI tools together help you?

Chapter 12: The Future of AI in Heavy Equipment Maintenance

As AI technology continues to evolve, the future for mechanics looks both exciting and challenging. AI won't just live on your phone or laptop—it will be embedded in your diagnostic tools, service trucks, and maybe even directly in your machines.

Predictive Maintenance Will Be Standard

With onboard sensors and telematics systems already gathering data, AI will become the brain that analyzes patterns in that data. Instead of waiting for a fault code, AI will alert you **before** failure happens.

Imagine this:

- Your machine's telematics feed is being watched by an AI trained on 10 million hours of excavator data.
- It notices rising exhaust temps and slightly delayed boost pressure.
- You get a message: "Potential turbo degradation – 90% confidence of failure in 40 hours."

This is the power of predictive AI.

AI-Driven OEM Portals

Expect manufacturers to integrate AI into service portals:

- Ask questions about a model and get targeted instructions
- Get interactive diagnostic trees
- Use AI to filter through thousands of TSBs and match them to symptoms

Augmented Reality and AI

Soon, you might point your phone or tablet at a machine, and AI will identify components, overlay procedures, and guide your hands through repairs. Already, apps are being tested for AR repair guides.

AI-Powered Training

Training simulations powered by AI will adapt in real-time to your knowledge level. If you struggle with electrical diagrams, it will give you extra practice. If you're learning regen systems, it will quiz you and offer instant feedback.

Better Workflows for Independent Mechanics

Independent techs will benefit from:

- AI-suggested parts sourcing based on location and price
- Drafted service invoices
- Customer-friendly repair summaries

AI can help you run a more professional shop without extra admin staff.

What It Won't Replace

- **Hands-on skill** – AI won't turn wrenches.
- **Judgment** – AI doesn't know your job site.
- **Experience** – AI lacks your instincts.

Mechanics who **embrace** AI as a tool, not a threat, will gain a serious edge.

Final Thoughts

The best mechanics of the next 20 years will be those who blend:

- Time-tested mechanical knowledge
- Strong troubleshooting logic
- Smart use of AI tools

You don't need to be a programmer. You just need to be curious and willing to learn.

Use this book as a starting point, and keep exploring.

Chapter Questions:

1. How will predictive maintenance change the way you approach repairs?
2. What are two examples of how AI might integrate with OEM portals?
3. Why is AI unlikely to ever replace experienced mechanics?

Chapter Questions:

1. How will predictive maintenance change the way you approach repairs?
2. What are two examples of how AI might integrate with OEM portals?
3. Why is AI unlikely to ever replace experienced mechanics?

Appendix A: SPEC Prompt Cheat Sheet

The SPEC Method is a fast and effective structure for crafting powerful AI prompts in the workshop. Keep this cheat sheet on hand when using AI during diagnostics or repair planning.

S – Specify Machine & System

Clearly identify the make, model, year, and the specific system or component you're referring to.

- Example: "2017 Komatsu PC360LC-11, swing motor hydraulic system."

P – Present the Problem or Symptoms

State what the issue is, including timing, triggers, and whether any codes are active.

- Example: "Swing is sluggish when warm. No active fault codes."

E – Elaborate with Important Context

Include hours, maintenance history, operating conditions, and any recent work done.

- Example: "8,200 hours. Hydraulic fluid changed 30 hours ago. Machine operates in dusty conditions."

C – Command a Clear Action and Format

Tell the AI exactly what you want it to do and how to format the answer.

- Example: "List top 5 likely causes in bullet form, with one test suggestion each."

Fast Prompt Template:

Act as a [Specialist Type]. Machine: [Make, Model, Year]. System: [System Name]. Symptom: [Detailed Issue]. Context: [Hours, recent service, environment]. Task: [What you want]. Format: [List, steps, summary, etc.]

This structured approach consistently delivers better answers and makes troubleshooting with AI faster and more reliable.

Appendix B: Glossary of Terms

AI (Artificial Intelligence): Machine systems designed to perform tasks like reasoning, learning, and problem-solving.

LLM (Large Language Model): A type of AI trained on huge amounts of text data that can generate human-like responses.

Prompt: The question or instruction you give an AI to generate a response.

OEM (Original Equipment Manufacturer): The company that built the machine—e.g., CAT, Komatsu, Deere.

SPN/FMI Codes: Diagnostic trouble codes used in J1939 systems to indicate system faults, with SPN identifying the parameter and FMI indicating the type of fault.

CAN Bus: A communication network that allows electronic control units (ECUs) in machinery to talk to each other without needing a separate wire for each function.

Hallucination (AI): When an AI confidently generates information that is incorrect, misleading, or entirely fabricated.

Predictive Maintenance: The practice of using data (from sensors, historical records, etc.) and AI to anticipate equipment failure before it occurs, allowing for proactive repairs.

Chain-of-Thought Prompting: A prompting technique where AI is asked to reason step-by-step rather than providing a single direct answer, often leading to more accurate outputs.

SPEC Method: A framework for writing effective prompts: Specify the machine and system, Present the symptoms, Elaborate with context, and Command an action/output format.

Appendix C: Recommended AI Tools & Resources

This appendix provides a curated list of helpful AI tools, communities, and OEM platforms that can enhance your skills, speed up diagnostics, and expand your learning.

Recommended AI Chatbots

ChatGPT (OpenAI)

- Best all-around reasoning and clarity
- Excellent for step-by-step diagnostics, checklists, and explanation prompts

Claude (Anthropic)

- Ideal for long documents, safety policies, or full technical bulletins
- Handles lots of context in one prompt

Gemini (Google)

- Best for integrated search queries
- Useful for up-to-date industry news or videos

Perplexity AI

- Great for sourced answers
- Fast and often includes references and article link

www.ingramcontent.com/pod-product-compliance
Lightning Source LLC
LaVergne TN
LVHW080106070326
832902LV00014B/2460